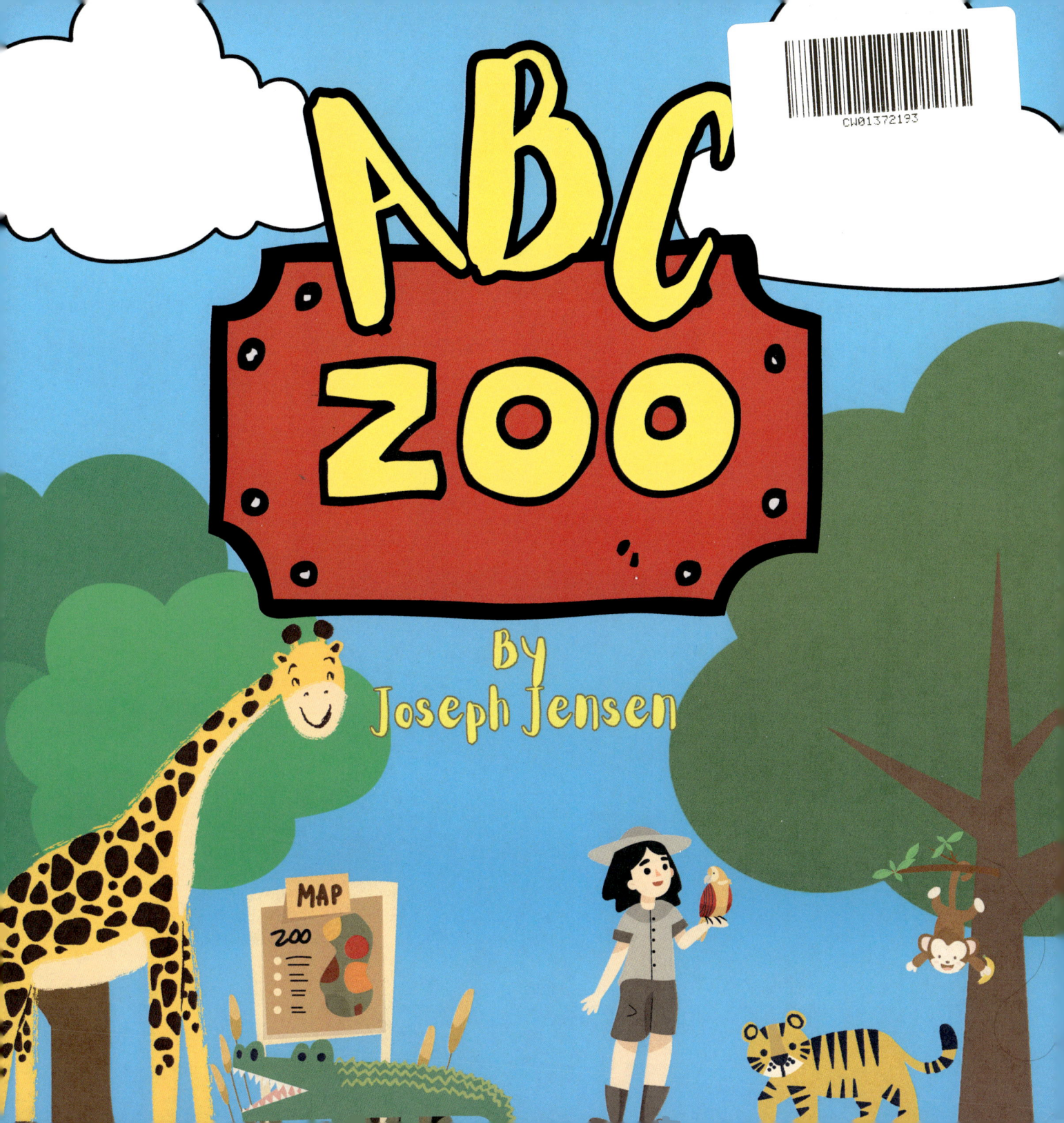

Copyright © 2023 by Joseph Jensen
All rights reserved.
No portion of this book may be reproduced in any form without written permission from the publisher or author, except as permitted by U.S. copyright law.

With each new letter, a new surprise,
A chance to learn and widen our eyes.
So come along, let's take a stroll,
Through the zoo, and explore them all!

Oh, look, it's a bear in a cave!
I think his name is Dave!
Big and brown,
the furriest creature in town.

Oh, look, it's a dolphin in a pool!

Making a splash and acting so cool!

DOLPHIN

Oh, look, it's a hippo!
Playing in the mud,
    looking so happy covered in crud!

HIPPO

Oh, look, it's an iguana so green!

Lounging on a rock like it's a queen!

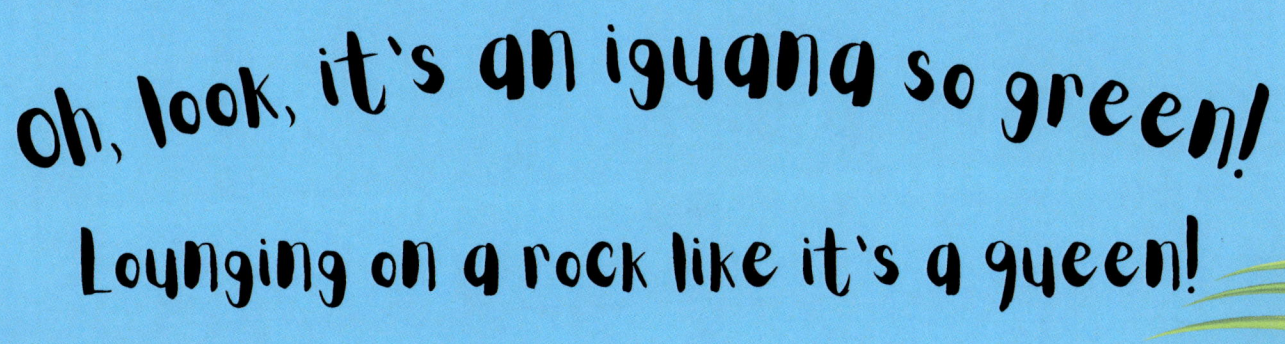

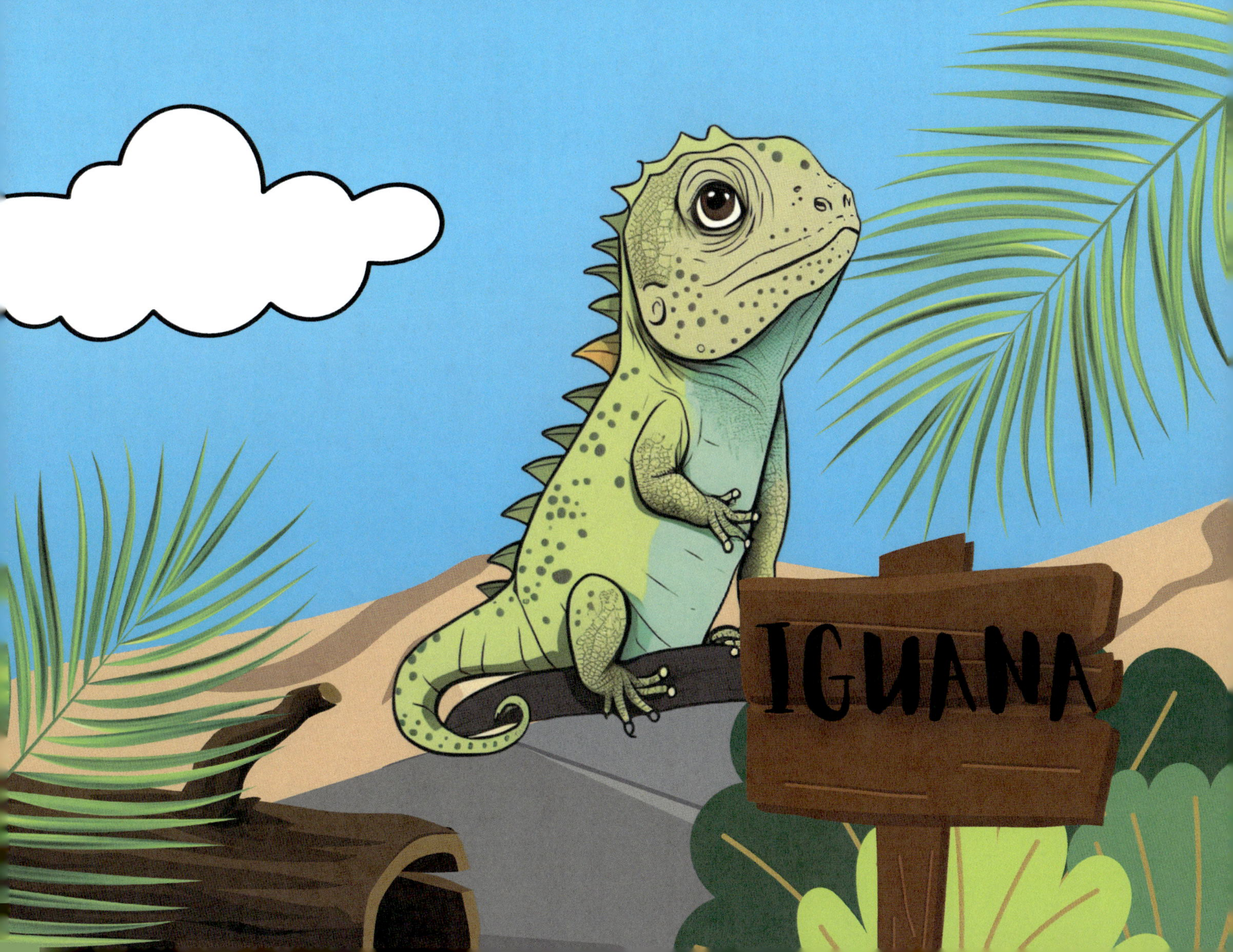

Oh, look, it's an orangutan!
with arms so strong and wide,
swinging through the trees
with ease and with pride!

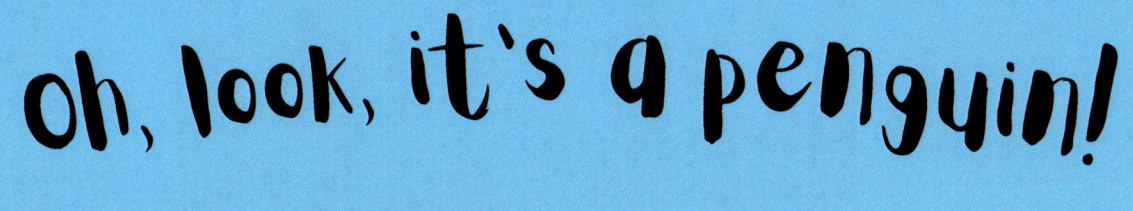

Oh, look, it's a penguin!
With feathers black and white,
waddling on the ice,
such a funny sight!

PENGUIN

We're walking through the zoo,
We're walking through the zoo,
What will we see?
What will we do?

Oh, look, it's a quokka!
With a smile on its face,
hopping around happily,
in its favorite place!

QUOKKA

We're walking through the zoo,

We're walking through the zoo,

What will we see?

What will we do?

Oh, look, it's a rhino!
With a horn on its head,
walking with such power,
like a king instead!

RHINO

We're walking through the zoo,
we're walking through the zoo,
what will we see?
what will we do?

Oh, look, it's a sloth!
Moving very slow,
 sleeping in a tree,
  while we walk below!

SLOTH

We're walking through the zoo,
we're walking through the zoo,
what will we see?
what will we do?

Oh, look, it's a tiger!
With stripes of orange and black,
lounging in the sun,
on a warm and cozy mat!

TIGER

We're walking through the zoo,
We're walking through the zoo,
What will we see?
What will we do?

Oh, look, it's an umbrellabird!
With a big and fluffy crest,
spreading out its feathers,
looking its best!

UMBRELLABIRD

We're walking through the zoo,
we're walking through the zoo,
What will we see?
What will we do?

Reptiles

Monkey House

Oh, look, it's a viper!

Slithering on the ground,
with scales so shiny,
moving without a sound!

VIPER

We're walking through the zoo,
we're walking through the zoo,
What will we see?
What will we do?

Oh, look, it's a wolf!

With fur so thick,
and a howl so loud,
their presence in the forest is felt all around!

WOLF

We're walking through the zoo,
we're walking through the zoo,
what will we see?
what will we do?

Oh, look, it's an x-ray fish!

A fish with skin, so see-through,
found in the Amazon,
a wonder to view!

X-RAY FISH

We're walking through the zoo,
We're walking through the zoo,
What will we see?
What will we do?

Oh, look, it's a yak!

With shaggy fur so thick,
 living in the mountains,
  such a unique pick!

YAK

We're walking through the zoo,
We're walking through the zoo,
What will we see?
What will we do?

Oh, look, it's a a zebra!
Like fingerprints are unique,
a zebra's a beauty,
you can never critique!

ZEBRA

The day is done, we had so much fun,

Let's take a moment to remember everyone!

From A to Z, let's name them all,

and cherish the memories, big and small.

The End

Thank you for joining us today,
On this adventure, come what may.
From A to Z, we explored with glee,
The wonders of nature, for all to see.

We hope you enjoyed this little trip,
And that you learned something new and hip.
So go outside, explore some more,
And let the wild world, your heart adore.

Remember to protect and care,
For all the creatures, big and rare.
And always keep in mind this rhyme,
To treasure nature, for all time.

Made in the USA
Monee, IL
15 May 2023